Fort Necessity National Battlefield and Friendship Hill National Historic Site

Weather of 2007

Natural Resource Data Series NPS/ERMN/NRDS—2010/076

Paul Knight, Tiffany Wisniewski, Chad Bahrmann, and Sonya Miller

Pennsylvania State Climate Office
503 Walker Building
Pennsylvania State University
University Park, Pennsylvania

September 2010

U.S. Department of the Interior
National Park Service
Natural Resource Program Center
Fort Collins, Colorado

The National Park Service, Natural Resource Program Center publishes a range of reports that address natural resource topics of interest and applicability to a broad audience in the National Park Service and others in natural resource management, including scientists, conservation and environmental constituencies, and the public.

The Natural Resource Data Series is intended for timely release of basic data sets and data summaries. Care has been taken to assure accuracy of raw data values, but a thorough analysis and interpretation of the data has not been completed. Consequently, the initial analyses of data in this report are provisional and subject to change.

All manuscripts in the series receive the appropriate level of peer review to ensure that the information is scientifically credible, technically accurate, appropriately written for the intended audience, and designed and published in a professional manner. This report received informal peer review by subject-matter experts who were not directly involved in the collection, analysis, or reporting of the data. Data in this report were collected and analyzed using methods based on established, peer-reviewed protocols and were analyzed and interpreted within the guidelines of the protocols.

Views, statements, findings, conclusions, recommendations, and data in this report do not necessarily reflect views and policies of the National Park Service, U.S. Department of the Interior. Mention of trade names or commercial products does not constitute endorsement or recommendation for use by the U.S. Government.

This report is available from Eastern Rivers and Mountains Network (http://science.nature.nps.gov/im/units/ERMN) and the Natural Resource Publications Management website (http://www.nature.nps.gov/publications/NRPM).

Please cite this publication as:

Knight, P., T. Wisniewski, C. Bahrmann, and S. Miller. 2010. Fort Necessity National Battlefield and Friendship Hill National Historic Site: Weather of 2007. Natural Resource Data Series NPS/ERMN/NRDS—2010/076. National Park Service, Fort Collins, Colorado.

NPS 336/105513, 476/105513, September 2010

Table of Contents

Figures

Tables

List of Key Acronyms

COOP   National Weather Service Cooperative Observer Program

CWOP   Citizen Weather Observer Program

ERMN   Eastern Rivers and Mountains Network

FAA   Federal Aviation Administration

FONE   Fort Necessity National Battlefield

FRHI   Friendship Hill National Historic Site

GOES   Geostationary Operational Environmental Satellite

IFLOWS   Integrated Flood Observing and Warning System

NADP   National Atmospheric Deposition Program

NARR   North American Regional Reanalysis

NB   National Battlefield

NCDC   National Climatic Data Center

NHS   National Historic Site

NOAA   National Oceanic and Atmospheric Administration

NWS   National Weather Service

PDSI   Palmer Drought Severity Index

POR   Period of Record

PRISM   Parameter-elevation Regressions on Independent Slopes Model

RAWS   Remote Automated Weather Stations

USDM   United States Drought Monitor

USGS   United States Geological Survey

Purpose of the Report

Weather and climate are widely recognized as key drivers of terrestrial and aquatic ecosystems affecting biotic as well as abiotic ecosystem characteristics and processes. Global and regional scale climatic patterns, trends, and variations are critical to the cycling of elements, nutrients, and minerals through the ecosystems and can deliver pollutants from regional and even global sources (National Assessment Synthesis Team 2001). These variations and trends influence the fundamental properties of ecologic systems such as soil-water relationships and plant-soil processes and their disturbance rates and intensity. Information obtained from meteorological monitoring will be useful to interpreting and understanding changes in species composition, community structure, water and soil chemistry, and related landscape processes (Marshall and Piekielek 2007).

The purpose of this report is to provide a concise weather and climate summary for January 1 to December 31, 2007, and to place current patterns and trends in an appropriate historical and regional context (Knight et al., in preparation). It is our intention that this report will satisfy an inherent interest in meteorological phenomena and meet the Eastern Rivers and Mountains Network (ERMN) Weather and Climate Monitoring objectives:

- Document long-term trends in weather and climate through seasonal and annual summaries of selected parameters (e.g., multiple forms of precipitation, temperature).
- Identify and document extremes and averages of climatic conditions for common parameters (e.g., precipitation, air temperature) and other parameters where sufficient data are available (e.g., wind speed and direction, solar radiation).
- Provide information on near real-time weather parameters, historical climate patterns, and climate station metadata from a single, easy-to-use Internet portal.

To accomplish these objectives, a variety of atmospheric data streams were evaluated for their quality, longevity, and applicability to the ERMN parks. Since no single weather observing network contains all the pertinent measures of atmospheric phenomena to assess ecosystem health, an objective analysis of the data networks was developed and outlined in the Weather and Climate Monitoring Protocol for the Eastern Rivers and Mountains Network and Mid-Atlantic Network of the National Park Service (Knight et al., in preparation). Through this analysis, a select number of weather/climate observing stations were chosen as representative of each park; these are the primary data sources used to profile climate summary and trends.

In addition to a suite of summary tables, graphs, and narratives, we specifically identify a series of key climatological indicators to report status and trends on an annual basis and periodically in separate and more thorough reports. These key indicators are further described in the protocol (Knight et al., in preparation) and summarized in the body of this report.

Weather Summary

Calendar year 2007 began very mild, but winter returned with persistent chill from mid-January until later February. A potent winter storm brought heavy snow and ice around St. Valentine's Day. Another bout of rather cold air was noted in April with unusually frequent snows. The heaviest rainstorm of the year occurred August 21, with some sections receiving more than 4.0 inches (11.0 cm) in one day. A relatively dry and mild time dominated much of the spring and summer. Very warm weather in September became the warmest October on record. November was cool and moist and the year concluded with cool, moist weather.

Long-term Trends

The lengthening of the growing season continues to be the most pronounced regional trend (Table 1). However, in 2007 this trend was exhibited by an average 'last' frost (about May 13) and a rather late first freeze (October 29). The trend toward milder winter nights did register a small setback in 2007, as a late January to mid-February cold snap produced several sub-zero mornings. A significant increase in rainfall was evident with a very wet August.

As cycles in ocean temperature anomalies shift, the longer-term effects of a change in water temperatures to lower (cool) values around the rim of the North Pacific adjacent to North America should impact autumn temperatures (warmer than usual September–October) as well as the frequency of cold air outbreaks during the winter in Pennsylvania (more often). A minimum in solar activity, often associated with a decrease in annual temperatures, was also noted in 2007.

Table 1. Summary of 2007 significant climate indicators for Friendship Hill National Historic Site and Fort Necessity National Battlefield.

Weather Indicator	2007 Statistics	Comments on Trends
Hot Days (Tmax>32°C/90°F)	11–19 days	Above the 30-year mean of 2–10 days
Cold Days(Tmax<0°C/32°F)	30–32 days	Near the 30-year mean of 24–45 days
Winter Minimums (Lowest Temp)	~ -20°C -4°F	Below the long-term average of -18°C -1°F
Growing Season: (Days between last 0°C/32°F in spring and first 0°C/32°F in fall)	166–199 days	Near the 30-year mean of 175–200 days
Total Precipitation (Calendar Year - inches)	36–42 inches	Below the average of 40–46 inches
Annual Snowfall (Calendar Year - inches)	23–26 inches	Below the 30-year mean of 45–70 inches

The Climate of the Southwest Plateau

Fort Necessity National Battlefield and Friendship Hill National Historic site are located in Pennsylvania Climate Division 9, also known as the "Southwest Plateau." A climate division is a region that is reasonably homogenous with respect to climatic and hydrologic characteristics and is frequently used for compiling climate statistics (http://www.esrl.noaa.gov/psd/data/usclimate/map.html). Pennsylvania is divided into 10 climate divisions.

The Southwest Plateau is generally considered to have a humid, continental type of climate, but the elevated terrain and rolling hills keep temperatures a bit lower than in surrounding areas. The prevailing westerly winds carry most of the weather disturbances that affect the region from the interior of the continent, with the Atlantic Ocean having only occasional influence on the climate of the area (Davey et al. 2007). Coastal storms do, at times, affect the day-to-day weather, especially in winter, though air circulating southeastward from the Great Lakes dominates in the winter. Seldom do storms of tropical origin have a direct effect in this part of Pennsylvania, but the rough terrain has led to memorable floods in the warm half of the year (Gelber 2002).

Temperatures are moderately continental, with the tempering effects of the Great Lakes contributing to cloud production in the winter and mountain-valley circulation-induced clouds reducing the heat during the summer. The lowest readings in the winter occur with polar air masses of Canadian origin settling over the Northeast after a fresh snowfall. The highest readings of summer happen when the sub-tropical fair weather system, the Bermuda high, pushes westward into the Carolinas; its clockwise circulation will direct hot, humid air from the Gulf region into the Laurel Highlands. Annual maximum and minimum temperatures tend to be greater in Friendship Hill NHS than in Fort Necessity NB. The average annual maximum temperature in Chalk Hill, PA is 54.4°F (12.4°C), while the annual maximum temperature in Grays Woods, PA is 63.4°F (17.4°C). The last freeze in the region typically occurs in early May and the first frosts appear in late September or October.

Precipitation is fairly evenly distributed throughout the year. Annual amounts generally range between 36–54 in (914–1,372 mm), while the majority of places receive 40–46 in (1,016–1,372 mm). Greatest amounts usually occur in the spring and summer months, while February is the driest month, having about 2.0 in (51 mm) less than the wettest months. Precipitation tends to be somewhat greater in the higher terrain due to uplift and additional moisture from the Great Lakes. Annual snowfall amounts are much greater for Fort Necessity NB than Friendship Hill NHS.

Surface winds blow from the west and northwest in the cold season and from the southwest during the warm half of the year. Thunderstorms follow a frequency matching the solar cycle between the equinoxes and reaching a peak near the summer solstice. Hail is relatively infrequent, but flash floods and damaging thunderstorm winds affect parts of the region each summer. On average, tornadoes pass through the area about once every two years. Ice storms, which can cause significant disruption, occur at irregular intervals and are primarily confined to the months between December and March (Kocin and Uccellini 2004).

Observing Stations

A total of six weather observing stations comprising five observing networks (Table 2) were selected around FONE and FRHI (Figure 1). The station identifiers in blue text (Figure 1) indicate those from which data has been used within this report. Stations that are not in blue text contain incomplete data for 2007 (Table 3). In addition to the summary information available in this report, a Web-interface is available that has a variety of data sources in near real-time (Figure 2).

Table 2. List of the five weather observing networks around Friendship Hill National Historic Site and Fort Necessity National Battlefield.

Network	Number of Stations
COOP	2
CASTNET	1
FAA	1
IFLOWS	1
GOES	1

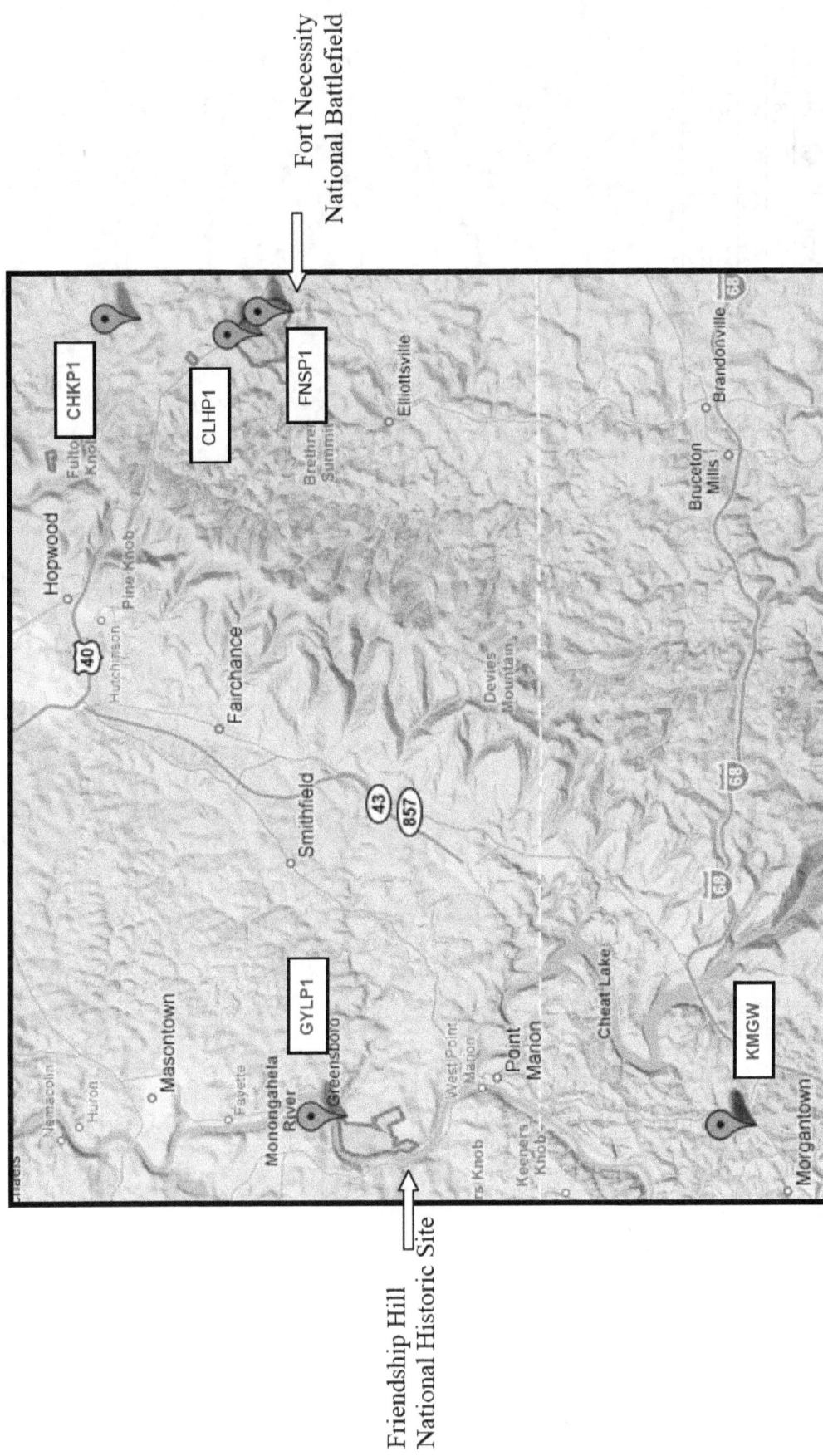

Figure 1. Location of weather observing stations around Friendship Hill National Historic Site and Fort Necessity National Battlefield. Not shown is the GOES station since its data was incomplete for 2007.

Table 3. List of weather observing stations around Friendship Hill National Historic Site and Fort Necessity National Battlefield. Those that are in bold have been selected as representative of the parks in large part dues to the percent time of reporting during 2007. Not all data networks are shown here – missing are the GOES and IFLOWS stations because their data were incomplete or not quality assured. The Laurel Hill precipitation data did not pass our quality assurance standard.

Stations	Network	Station Name	Period of Record (POR)		Percentage of Time Reporting Temperature for 2007	Percentage of Time Reporting Precipitation for 2007	Percentage of Time Reporting Temperature for entire POR	Percentage of Time Reporting Precipitation for entire POR
KMGW	FAA	Morgantown	1974-01-01	Present	**98.6**	**98.6**	28.5	28.5
CHKP1	COOP	Chalk Hill	1977-07-01	Present	**100.0**	**100.0**	99.3	99.3
GYLP1	COOP	Grays Landing	1996-10-01	Present	**100.0**	**100.0**	93.2	98.2
LRL117	CASTNET	Laurel Hill	1988-01-01	Present	**100.0**	100.0	100.0	100.0

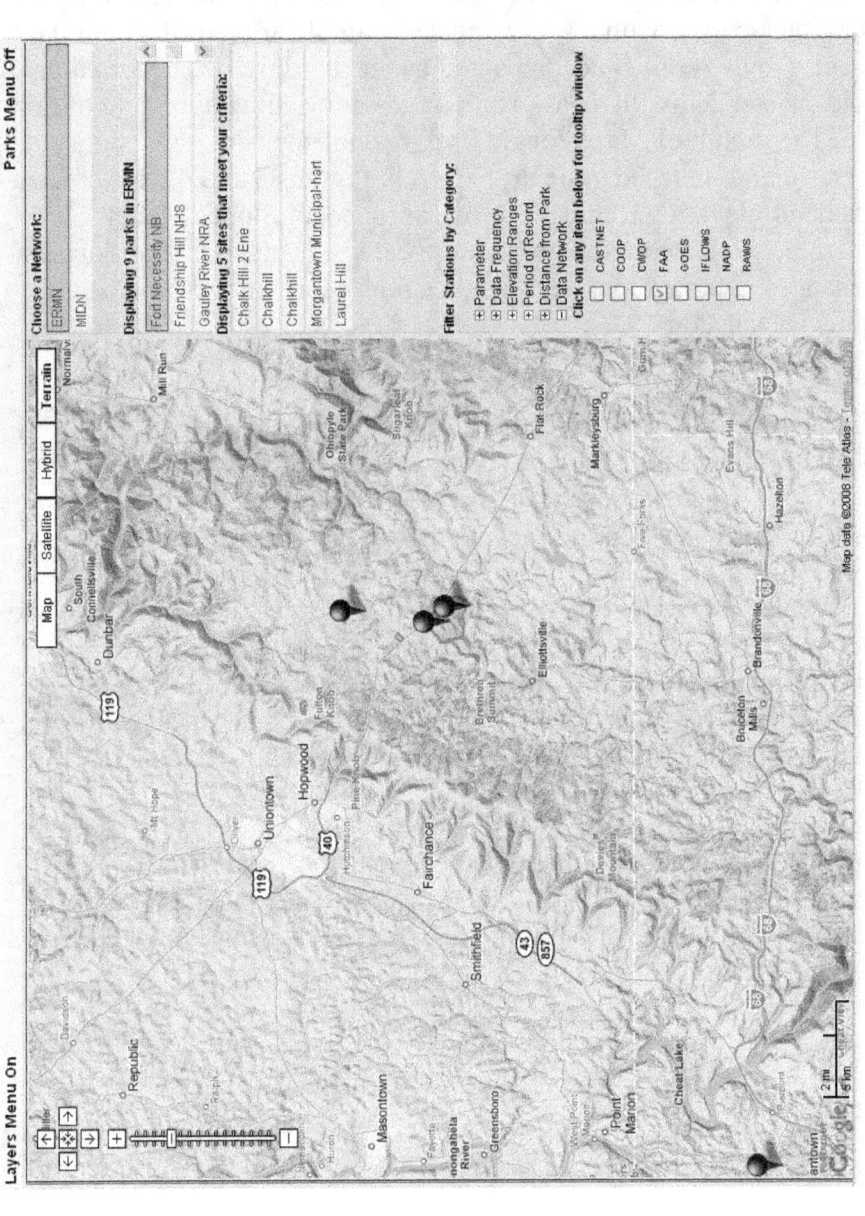

Figure 2. A snapshot of the Web-interface that is available at http://climate.met.psu.edu/gmaps/NPS_DEVELOPMENT/interface.php/.

Temperature Summary

Calendar year 2007 began, as many Januarys have during the most recent decade, with rather mild and moist weather (Figures 3 and 4, Tables 4 and 5). However, at mid-month wintry conditions returned and stayed consistently through mid-February. The winter's heaviest snowfall came around St. Valentine's Day when between 4 and 12 in (10 and 30 cm) of snow fell in the Laurel Highlands with similar amounts in the Southwest Plateau. The bitter chill gave way to a more seasonable chill interspersed with a few warm spells until early April. A ten-day period of unseasonably cold and snowy weather accompanied by late hard freezes occurred in the first half of April. The cold snap ended with a powerful nor'easter bringing a mixture of rain and wet snow on April 15–16. The month of May brought back several spells of very cool weather, but regular rainfall ended and it turned quite dry. Maps in Figures 3 and 4 were created using estimates from the Parameter-elevation Regressions on Independent Slopes Model (PRISM). PRISM uses an interpolation scheme for temperature between actual observations and corrects these estimates for changes in topography across the region. More information can be found at: http://www.prism.oregonstate.edu/.

Summer of 2007 had several short episodes of hot weather from May 23–June 3, July 29–Aug 14 (1 embedded cool day), and Aug 21–31. Oddly, the most anomalously warm weather did not occur until September 21–October 9, when readings averaged more than 7°F (3.5°C) degrees above the long-term mean for this three-week period. Several periods of showers dropped readings back to seasonal levels in mid-October. Regardless, autumn of 2007 was the 24th warmest in the last 114 years (Table 6). The first frosts were scattered around on October 13 and a widespread freeze was noted on October 29. November and December were marked by alternating cool and warm spells, though the mild spells lasted longer and the result was both months averaged slightly above normal (Figures 3 and 4). The season's first snowfall came in the higher elevation on November 7 and widespread snow on November 15. The year concluded with two weeks of mild weather.

The frequency of cold days (Tmax below freezing) was a bit above the 30-year mean, though the number of below-freezing nights was below the 1971–2000 mean. Sustained heat was noted by 18 days exceeding 90°F compared with the mean of three (though there is a substantial elevation difference between these stations) (Table 7).

The temperature trend since 1978 is upward at a rate of about 1.0°F (0.56°C) per decade (Figure 5).

Friendship Hill NB and Fort Necessity NHS
Departure from Average Monthly Maximum Temperature
2007 vs. 1971–2000

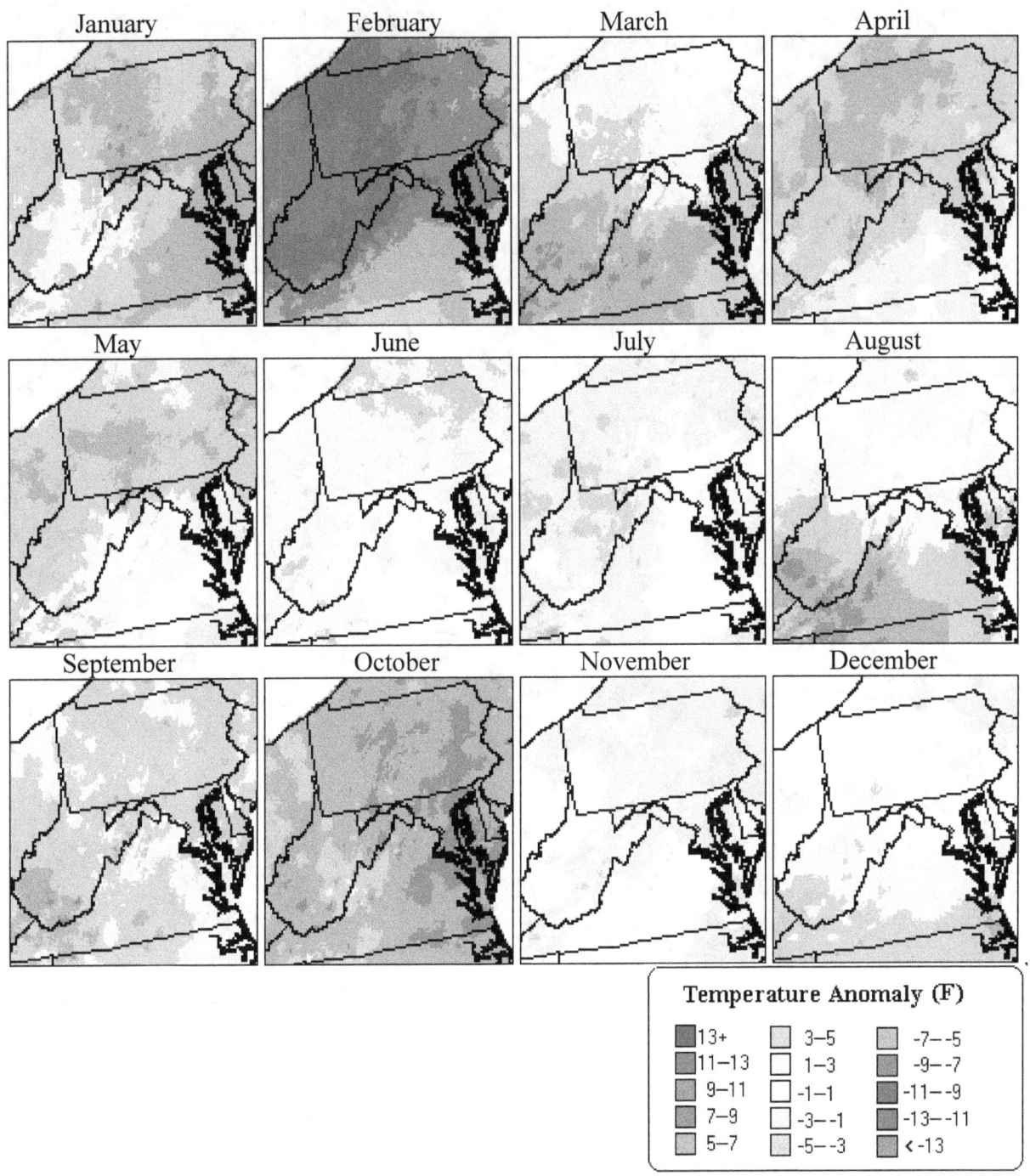

Figure 3. Maps showing departures from average maximum daily temperatures for each month in calendar year 2007 as compared with the normal based on the period 1971–20

Friendship Hill NB and Fort Necessity NHS
Departure from Average Monthly Minimum Temperature
2007 vs. 1971–2000

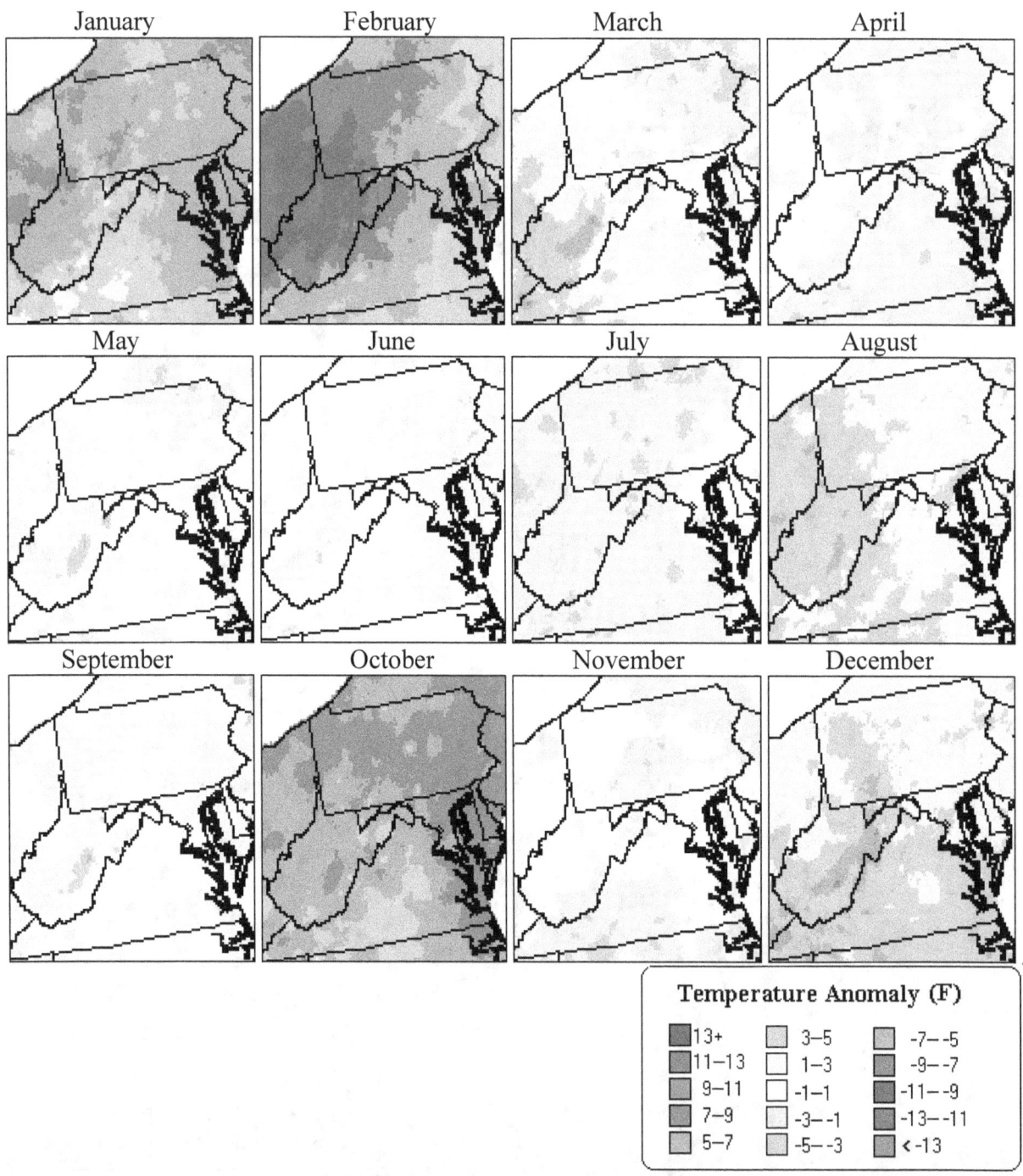

Figure 4. Maps showing departures from average minimum temperatures for each month in calendar year 2007 as compared with the normal based on the period 1971–2000.

Table 4. Summary of monthly average temperatures for 2007 from reporting sites that represent Friendship Hill National Historic Site and Fort Necessity National Battlefield.

Station Location	ID	ID Number	Jan	Feb	Mar	Apr	May	Jun	Jul	Aug	Sep	Oct	Nov	Dec	Annual
Chalk Hill 2 ENE, PA	CHKP1	361350	-0.48°C	-6.99°C	4.89°C	7.57°C	15.75°C	18.81°C	18.97°C	21.01°C	17.29°C	13.63°C	4.96°C	0.85°C	9.69°C
			31.13°F	19.41°F	40.81°F	45.62°F	60.35°F	65.85°F	66.15°F	69.84°F	63.13°F	56.53°F	40.92°F	33.53°F	49.44°F
Morgantown, WV	KMGW		2.47°C	-4.14°C	8.35°C	10.11°C	18.56°C	21.61°C	21.61°C	24.21^d°C	20.46°C	16.23°C	7.37°C	3.43°C	11.46°C
			36.45°F	24.54°F	47.03°F	50.19°F	65.40°F	70.89°F	70.89°F	75.57^d°F	68.82°F	61.22°F	45.26°F	38.18°F	52.62°F
Grays Landing, PA	GYLP1	363451	1.45°C	-5.81°C	5.66°C	8.40°C	16.68°C	20.72°C	20.92°C	23.58°C	19.37°C	15.39°C	5.79°C	1.59°C	11.14°C
			34.61°F	24.54°F	42.18°F	47.12°F	62.02°F	69.30°F	69.66°F	74.44°F	66.87°F	59.71°F	42.42°F	34.87°F	52.06°F
Laurel Hill, PA	LRL117		-1.07°C	-7.31°C	3.34°C	6.28°C	14.89°C	16.99°C	17.75°C	19.38°C	13.11°C	7.76°C	1.26°C	-0.40°C	7.67°C
			30.08°F	18.85°F	38.01°F	43.31°F	58.80°F	62.59°F	63.96°F	66.88°F	55.59°F	45.97°F	34.26°F	31.28°F	45.80°F

a = 1 day is missing, b = 2 days missing, c = 3 days missing, d = 4 days missing
Monthly statistics not reported if more than 4 days are missing

Table 5. Summary of departure from normal temperature based on 30-year normal (1971–2000) for 2007 from reporting sites that represent Friendship Hill National Historic Site and Fort Necessity National Battlefield.

Station Location	ID	ID Number	Jan	Feb	Mar	Apr	May	Jun	Jul	Aug	Sep	Oct	Nov	Dec
Chalk Hill 2 ENE, PA	CHKP1	361350	2.78°C	-5.39°C	1.62°C	-1.38°C	1.70°C	0.53°C	-1.37°C	1.47°C	1.46°C	3.63°C	0.51°C	1.51°C
			5.00°F	-9.70°F	2.91°F	-2.48°F	3.06°F	0.95°F	-2.46°F	2.65°F	2.63°F	6.53°F	0.92°F	2.72°F
Morgantown, WV	KMGW		3.48°C	-4.86°C	2.74°C	-0.84°C	2.39°C	1.16°C	-1.12°C	2.20°C	2.14°C	4.12°C	0.64°C	1.82°C
			6.26°F	-8.75°F	4.93°F	-1.51°F	4.30°F	2.09°F	-2.01°F	3.96°F	3.92°F	7.41°F	1.16°F	3.28°F

Table 6. Seasonal temperature and precipitation rankings over 114 years for PA Climate Division 9 for 2007. The values show cooler and drier than normal weather in the winter and spring, but the summer and autumn were quite wet (August being the wettest month).

Climate Division Rankings (Division 9)	Jan–Feb–Mar (Winter)	Apr–May–Jun (Spring)	Jul–Aug–Sep (Summer)	Oct–Nov–Dec (Autumn)
Temperature 2007	67	74	72	24
Precipitation 2007	62	84	21	28

1=Warmest or Wettest; 114 = Coldest or Driest

Table 7. Status of 2007 temperature indicators using the Morgantown, WV station (KMGW) compared to the 30-year normal (1971–2000) at the Elkins, WV (KEKN) station.

2007 Statistics Compared with 30-year Means	Morgantown, WV (KMGW) 2007	Elkins, WV (KEKN) 1971–2000
Number of days with Tmax <=0°C/32°F	29	27.3
Number of days with Tmin <=0°C/32°F	94	145.3
Number of days with Tmin <=-17°C/0°F	2	8.5
Number of days with Tmax >=32°C/90°F	18	3.1
Number of days between last 0°C/32°F in Spring and first 0°C/32°F in Fall	199	175–200

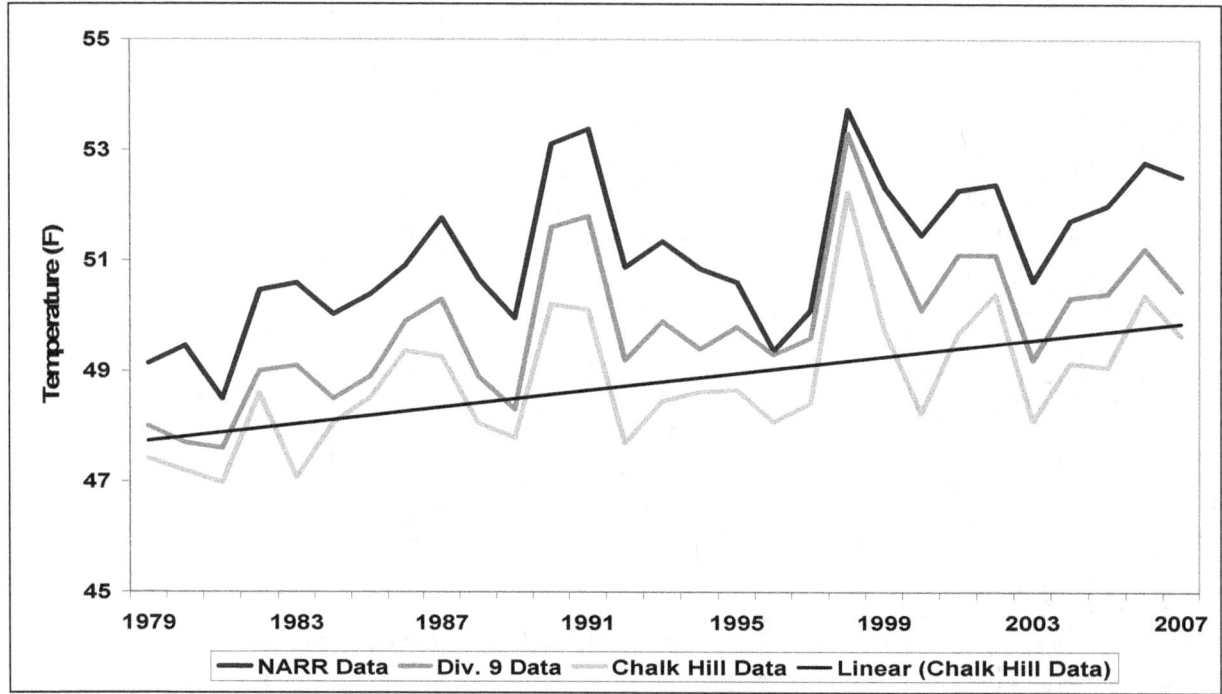

Figure 5. Annual temperature trends for Friendship Hill National Historic Site and Fort Necessity National Battlefield as seen by three distinct data sources. The red line shows PA climate division 9 data which is composed of more than six climate stations in the Pennsylvania counties adjacent to the park. The dark blue line is the temperature trend for a 32-km square box around Friendship Hill National Historic Site and Fort Necessity National Battlefield as derived from the North American Regional Reanalysis data set (NARR). This gridded database was the initial conditions for the numerical weather prediction models. The light blue shows the trend from a single Cooperative (COOP) weather station at Chalk Hill. The agreement between all three data sources indicates the reliability of the NARR data as a good proxy for actual park observations. The temperature trend is upward at a rate of about 0.56°C (1.0°F) per decade.

Precipitation Summary

January averaged near-normal precipitation and February was drier than normal across the region (Figure 6; Tables 8 and 9). In spite of near-normal precipitation, snowfall tallied above normal for this period, since much of the precipitation fell as snow from mid-January until the third week of February. The most significant winter storm of the season occurred just before St. Valentine's Day, with all sections receiving more than 6 in (15 cm) of snow and some measuring a foot or more (>30 cm). A wedge of mild air trapped in the storm circulation brought an icy mixture for many sections. March brought near-normal rain and snowfall, but April featured rather wet weather centered on a powerful nor'easter on April 15 (Table 10). After about 1.37 inches (35 mm) of rain, heavy, wet snow fell in the mountains.

The warm season of 2007 started and ended with very dry conditions (Figure 6). After a very wet April, May saw significant rainfall on only a handful of days. More routine showers and thunderstorms returned in June, but the scattered nature of this rain left most sections with a deficit. A bout of heavy thunderstorms in later July brought several reports of severe weather (Appendix). August had several periods of heavy thunderstorms which caused flash flooding in some sections. Then from late August until early October rainfall was sparse with no contribution of moisture from the Tropics. Three long, dry spells occurred during this period (Table 10). Rain returned in earnest starting on October 9, and within three weeks much of the region had received near-average rainfall. November was a bit wetter and December had above-normal snowfall and was wetter than normal, resulting in the 21st wettest summer (July–September) and 28th wettest autumn (October–December) in the past 114 years (Table 6).

The annual snowfall and the frequency of 1-inch snowfall were both well below normal, even with the elevation differential between Morgantown and Elkins, (Table 11) and the 30-year trend shows an increase of nearly 7% (3 in [76 mm]) since 1979 (Figure 7).

Maps showing percent of average precipitation for each month in calendar year 2007, as compared with the normal based on the period 1971–2000, are shown in Figure 6. Departure values are reported in percent of normal. Maps were created using estimates from the Parameter-elevation Regressions on Independent Slopes Model (PRISM). PRISM uses an interpolation scheme for precipitation between actual observations and corrects these estimates for changes in topography across the region. More information can be found at http://www.prism.oregonstate.edu/.

Friendship Hill NHS and Fort Necessity NB
Percent of Average Monthly Precipitation
2007 vs. 1971–2000

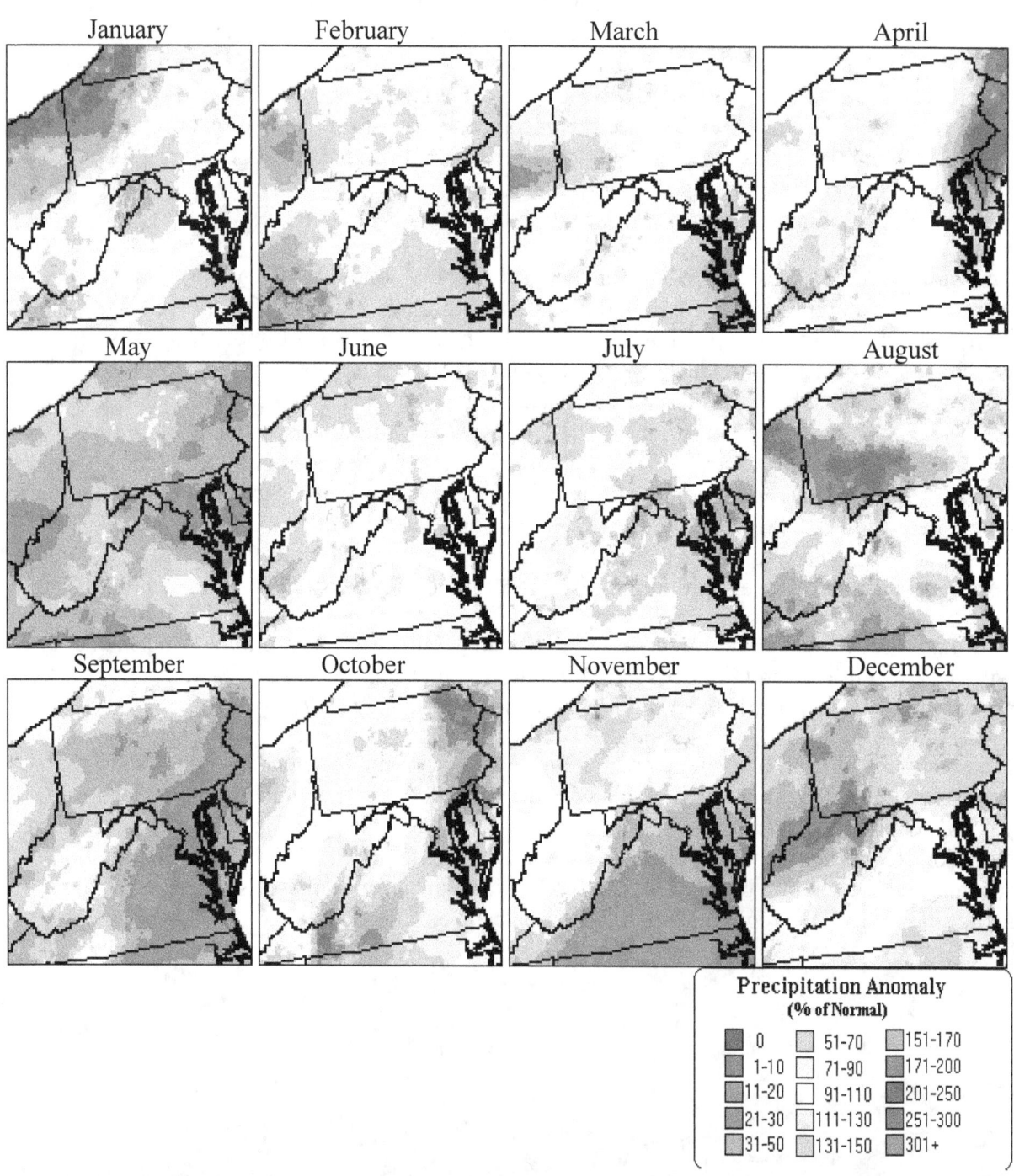

Figure 6. Maps showing percent of average precipitation for each month in the calendar year 2007 as compared with the normal based on the period 1971–2000.

Table 8. Summary of precipitation in 2007 for reporting sites that represent.

Station Location	ID	ID Number	Jan	Feb	Mar	Apr	May	Jun	Jul	Aug	Sep	Oct	Nov	Dec	Annual
Chalk Hill 2 ENE, PA	CHKP1	361350	12.93 cm	7.75 cm	16.66 cm	13.11 cm	6.32 cm	13.92 cm	12.62 cm	27.28 cm	6.43 cm	7.65 cm	11.00 cm	22.45 cm	158.12 cm
			5.09 in	3.05 in	6.56 in	5.16 in	2.49 in	5.48 in	4.97 in	10.74 in	2.53 in	3.01 in	4.33 in	8.84 in	62.25 in
Grays Landing, PA	GYLP1	363451	7.67 cm	4.09 cm	12.12 cm	8.92[a] cm	4.75 cm	6.20[b] cm	6.88 cm	19.02 cm	5.23 cm	5.18 cm	9.14 cm	14.83 cm	104.04 cm
			3.02 in	1.61 in	4.77 in	3.51[a] in	1.87 in	2.44[b] in	2.71 in	7.49 in	2.06 in	2.04 in	3.60 in	5.84 in	40.96 in
Morgantown, WV	KMGW		6.12 cm	2.74 cm	8.41 cm	10.57 cm	2.95[a] cm	7.65 cm	13.16 cm	12.40[d] cm	1.40 cm	6.63 cm	7.24 cm	12.75 cm	92.00 cm
			2.41 in	1.08 in	3.31 in	4.16 in	1.16[a] in	3.01 in	5.18 in	4.88[d] in	0.55 in	2.61 in	2.85 in	5.02 in	36.22 in

a = 1 day is missing, b = 2 days missing, c = 3 days missing, d = 4 days missing
Monthly statistics not reported if more than 4 days are missing

Table 9. Summary of 2007 percent of normal precipitation based on 30-year normal (1971–2000) for reporting sites that represent.

Station Location	ID	ID Number	Jan	Feb	Mar	Apr	May	Jun	Jul	Aug	Sep	Oct	Nov	Dec	Annual
Chalk Hill 2 ENE, PA	CHKP1	361350	118	81	140	103	48	115	90	252	56	82	103	217	115
Morgantown, WV	KMGW		84	53	89	118	40	73	123	121	62	92	85	164	86
Grays Landing	GYLP1	363451	92	73	130	98	45	60	72	196	71	153	114	229	103

Table 10. A comparison of wettest single calendar days during 2007 with the longest periods with a trace or less of rainfall during the same year.

Wettest Days in 2007	Dry Spells in 2007
21-Aug: 11.8 cm (4.64 in)	Aug 27–Sept 9
29-Jun: 6.0 cm (2.36 in)	Sep 29–Oct 5
13-Dec: 4.7 cm (1.86 in)	Sep 16–Sep 26
15-Jul: 3.7 cm (1.56 in)	Jul 29–Aug 5
6-Aug: 3.8 cm (1.50 in)	May 7–May 16
15-Apr: 3.5 cm (1.37 in)	May 30–Jun 3
23-Mar: 3.4 cm (1.33 in)	Feb 4–Feb 8

Table 11. Summary of the climate for FONE-FRHI as represented by hourly and daily summaries from the FAA site at Morgantown, West Virginia (KMGW). The thirty-year normal values for Elkins, West Virginia (KEKN) are used as a reference for establishing trends because of gaps present in long-term data from KMGW.

2007 Statistics Compared with 30 year Means	Morgantown, WV (KMGW) 2007	Elkins, WV (KEKN) 1971–2000
2007 Snowfall	22.3	80.5
Number of days >=2.5 cm (1.0 in) rain	8	6.7
Number of days with >=2.5 cm (1.0 in) snow	5	25.6
Number of days with thunderstorms	44	36.2

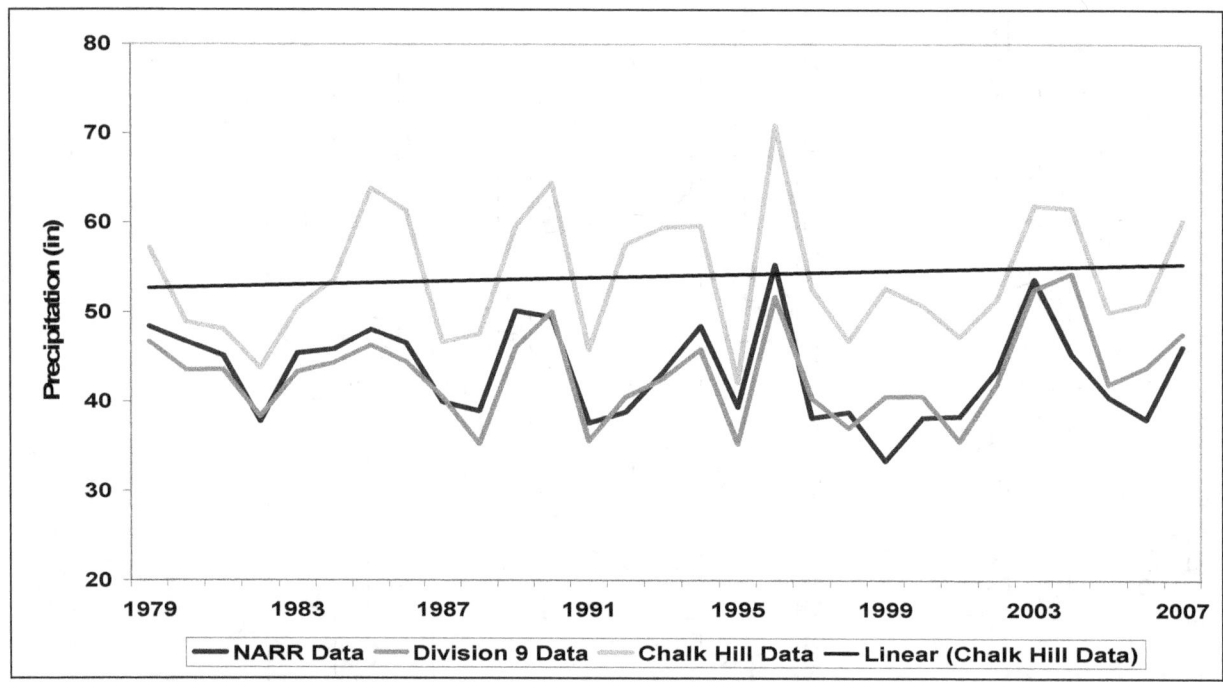

Figure 7. Annual precipitation trends for FONE/FRHI are shown by three separate lines. The red line tracks the climate division data (Div #9 in Pennsylvania) which represents an aggregate of more than six sites near the park. The dark blue line marks the trend of a grid box within FONE/FRHI from a North American Reanalysis data set. The light blue line shows the annual precipitation for a nearby single Cooperative weather station (COOP) at Chalk Hill, PA. The 30-year trend shows an increase of nearly 7% (about 3 in [76.2 mm]) since 1979.

16

Drought Status

The U.S. Drought Monitor (USDM; http://www.drought.unl.edu/dm/monitor.html) tracks drought conditions across the nation on a weekly basis and it incorporates data and expert input from a wide variety of state and federal agencies. The USDM is designed to represent a "broad brush," regional perspective (e.g., summarized by climate division, state, or region) on drought, and therefore provides an ideal tool for tracking generalized drought conditions across the central section of West Virginia and the enclosed parks. One index used to track drought conditions, the Palmer Drought Severity Index (PDSI), uses temperature and rainfall information to determine dryness (the long-term average is "zero"). Since the PDSI responds to long-term effects, including evaporation, there is usually a lag between both long dry spells and episodes of heavy rain and changes in the index value.

According to the USDM, the Palmer Drought Severity Index (PDSI) dropped from slightly moist (~ +1) during January–April to slightly dry (~ -1) by June (Figure 8). These conditions persisted into the summer and then rose again as wet weather returned in August, alleviating pockets of drought in the region. When compared with the past few years, the dry early summer of 2007 was akin to 2005, though this past year had more frequent showers in July and August. Comparative data is illustrated for Pennsylvania (Figure 9) and the Northeast (Figure 10).

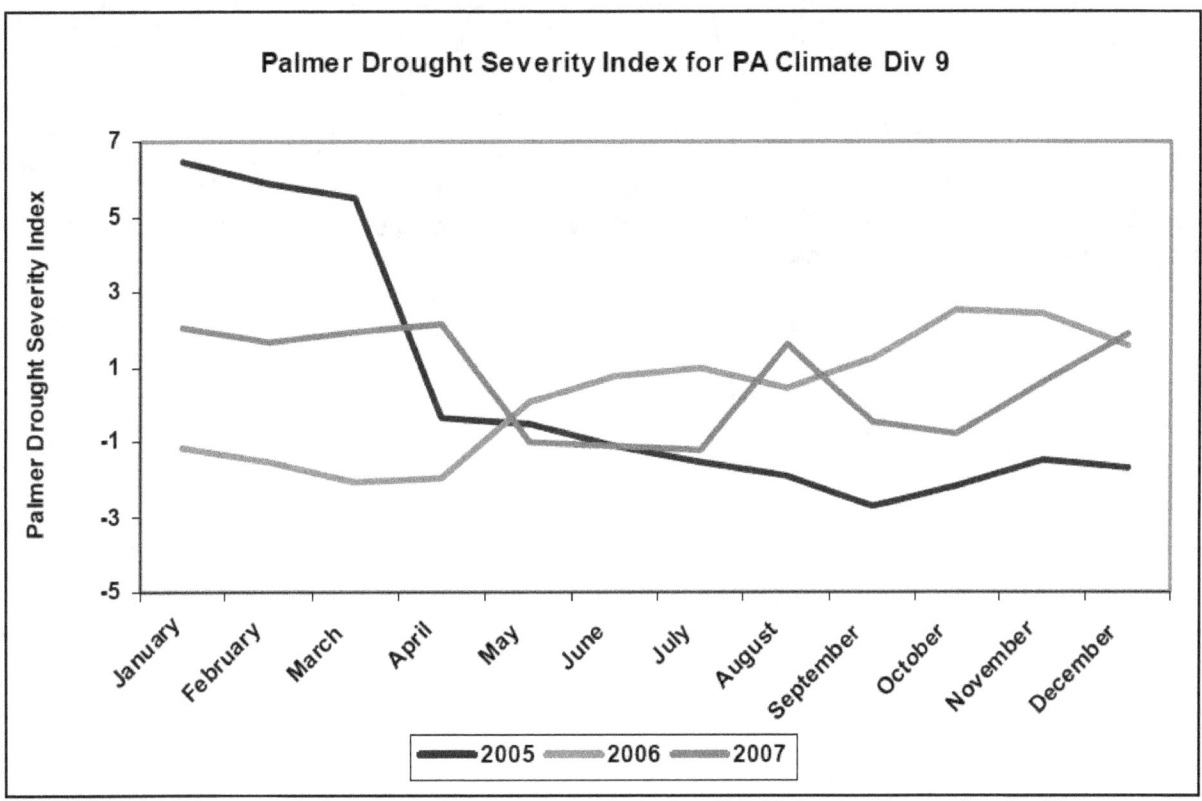

Figure 8. A comparison of the Palmer Drought Severity Index (PDSI) for the Pennsylvania Climate Division encompassing FONE-FRHI and the majority of the Southwest Plateau. The PDSI during 2007 was the closest to normal of the past three years.

Drought Severity in Pennsylvania during 2007

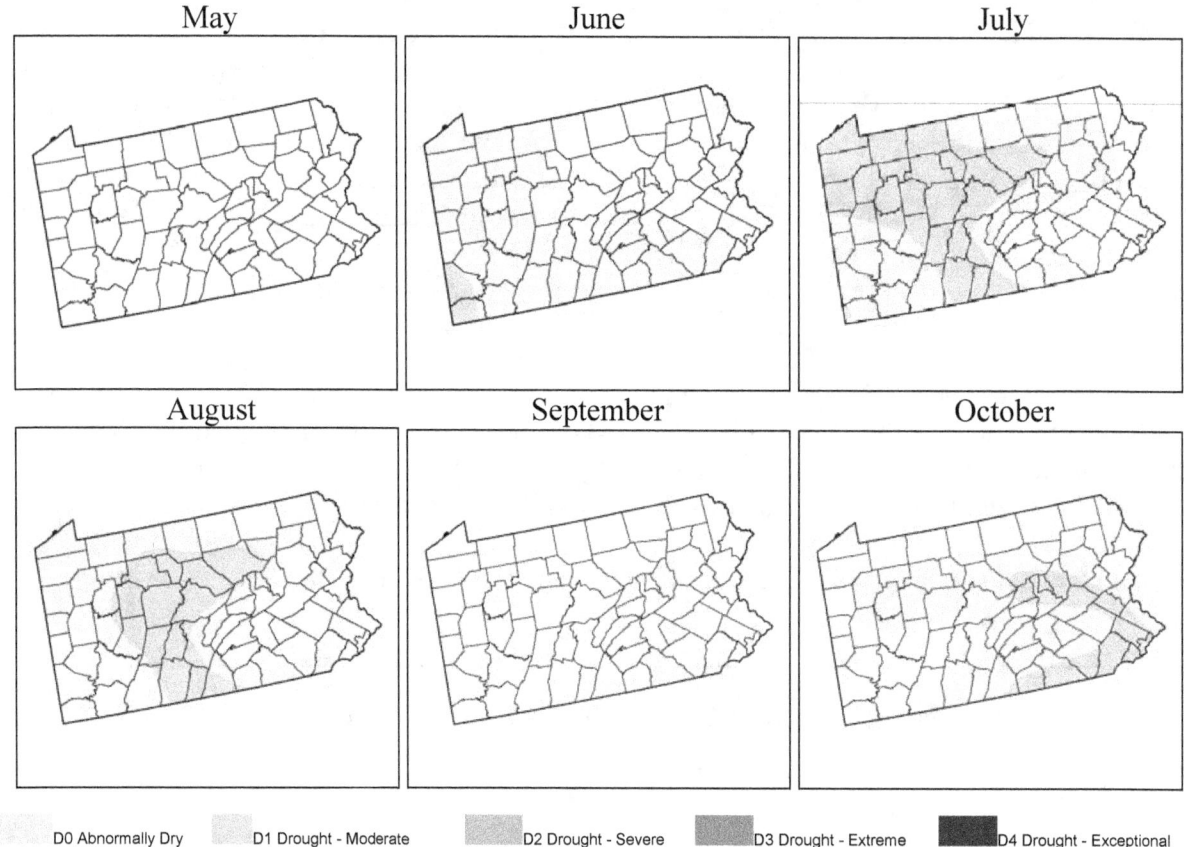

Figure 9. The mid-month values of the PDSI for Pennsylvania showing that dry conditions encroached on the Southwest Plateau Parks, especially in July.

Drought Severity for the Northeast during 2007

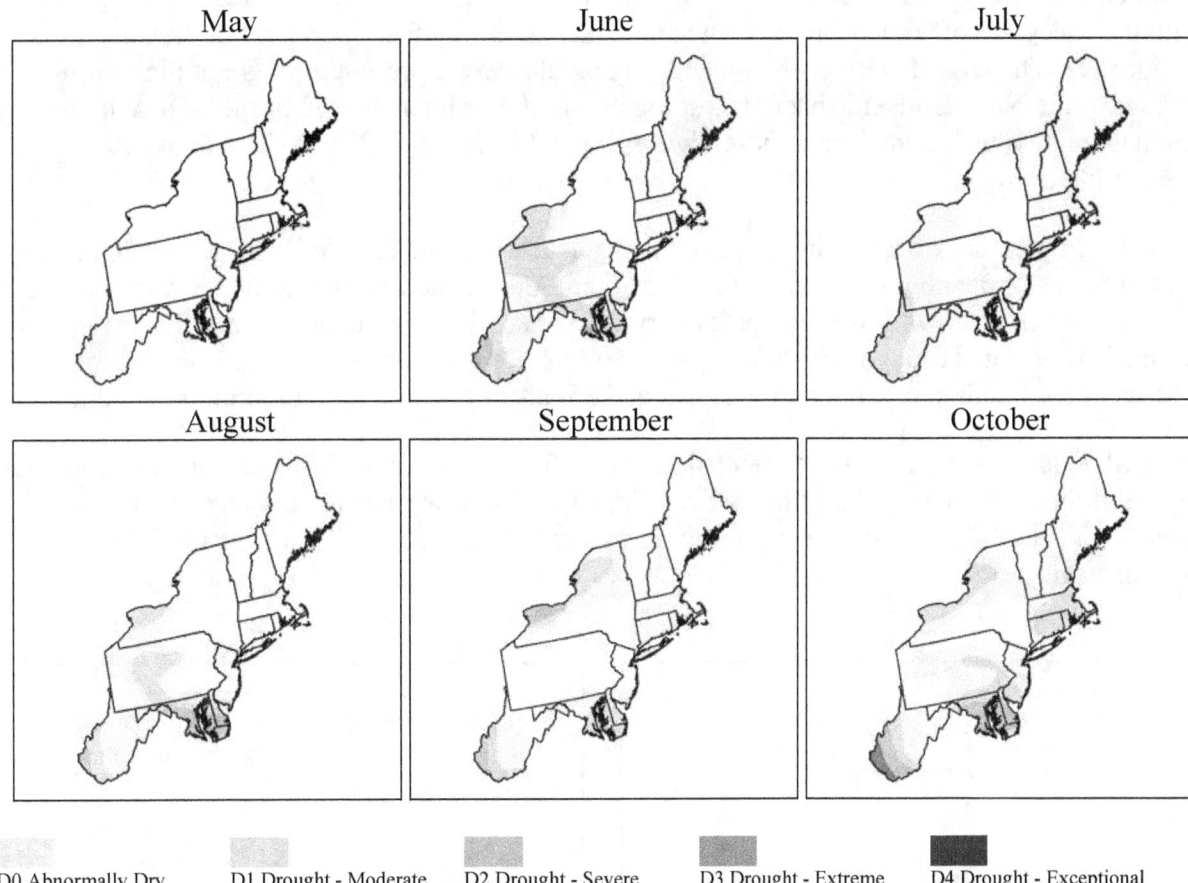

D0 Abnormally Dry   D1 Drought - Moderate   D2 Drought - Severe   D3 Drought - Extreme   D4 Drought - Exceptional

Figure 10. The mid-month values of the PDSI for the Northeast during the 2007 warm season. The Chesapeake Bay area was the most consistently dry region.

Global and National Summary

Warmer-than-average temperatures occurred throughout 2007 in most land areas of the world, with the exception of cooler-than-average anomalies in the southern parts of South America (Figure 11). The largest warmer-than-average anomalies were present throughout high-latitude regions of the Northern Hemisphere including much of North America, Europe, and Asia. Annual temperature anomalies in these regions ranged from 3.6–7.2°F (2–4°C) above the 1961–1990 average.

Notable temperature extremes in 2007 included a heat wave that affected a large portion of the United States throughout the month of August. The Central and Southeastern U.S. were particularly affected, with over 50 deaths attributed to soaring high temperatures. The anomalous warmth exacerbated drought conditions in the Southeastern region and also contributed for 29 all-time record high maximum temperatures and 35 all-time record high minimum temperatures.

In April, a devastating cold wave affected much of the central Plains, Midwest, and the Southeast region of the contiguous U.S. Temperatures dipped well below freezing in many areas, prompting nearly 1,240 broken daily minimum temperature records and producing significant crop damages.

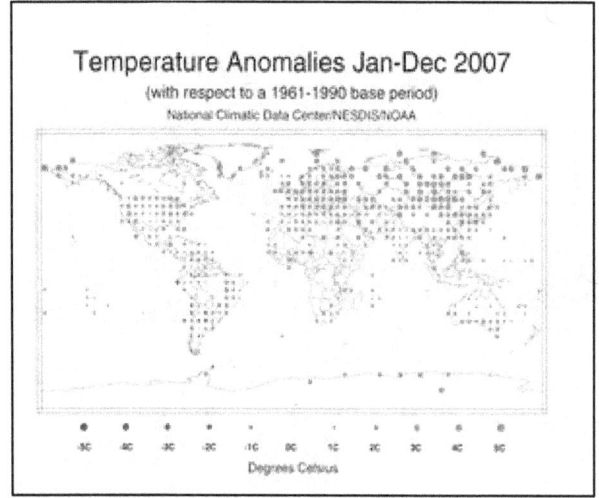 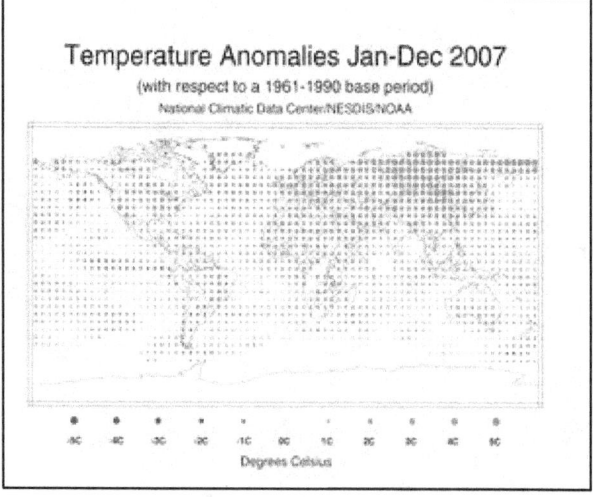

Annual Land Temperature Anomalies in degrees C

Annual Blended Land and Sea Temperature Anomalies in degrees C

Figure 11. Global temperature anomalies for 2007 with respect to a 1961–1990 base period. The map on left is created using data from the Global Historical Climatology Network (GHCN), a network of more than 7,000 land surface observing stations. The map on right is a product of a merged land surface and sea surface temperature anomaly analysis developed by Smith and Reynolds (2005). Temperature anomalies with respect to the 1961–1990 mean for land and ocean are analyzed separately and then merged to form the global analysis.

Snow cover for boreal winter 2007 across North America was above average and was the 13th largest extent over the 41-year historical record (Figure 12). This was, in part, due to a series of snow and ice storms that struck the U.S. during the month of February. Average North America boreal winter snow cover extent is 17.0 million square kilometers for the 1967–2007 period of record.

Mean Northern Hemisphere snow cover extent during boreal spring (March–May) 2007 was below average (Figure 13). Much of this was due to anomalously warm conditions across Asia, Europe, and most of the contiguous U.S. Spring 2007 snow cover extent on the Northern Hemisphere was the third lowest extent on record. Mean Northern Hemisphere spring snow cover extent for the 1997–2007 period of record is 92.6 million square kilometers.

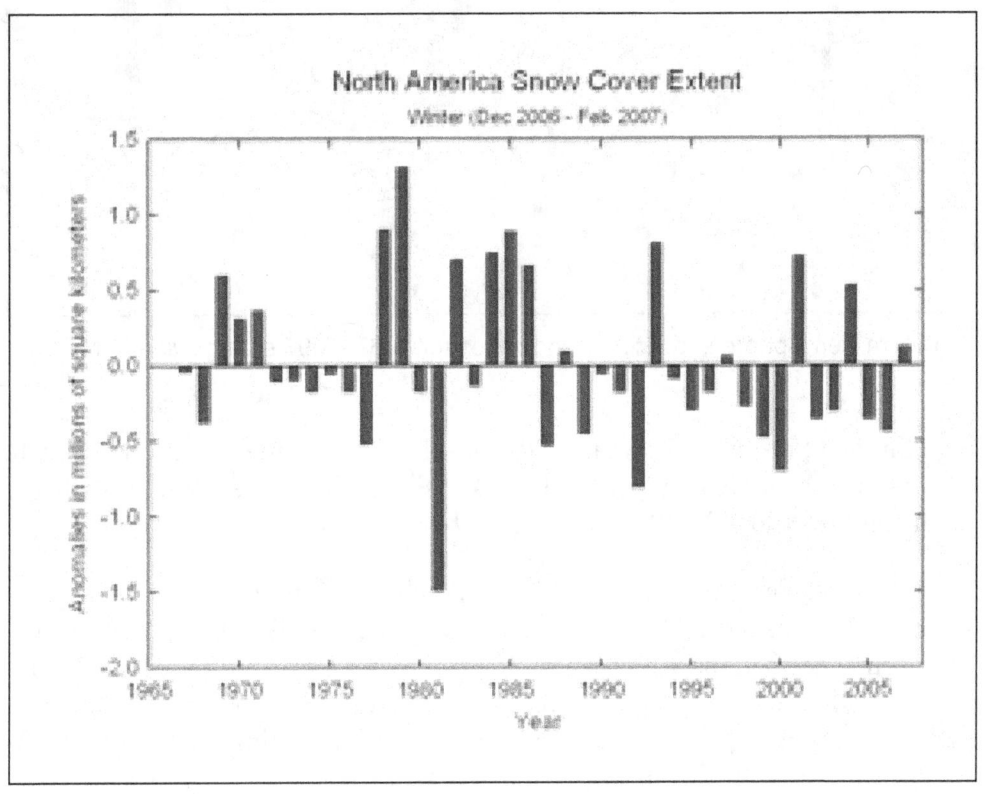

Figure 12. North American snow cover anomalies for 1967–2007 winters (December–February).

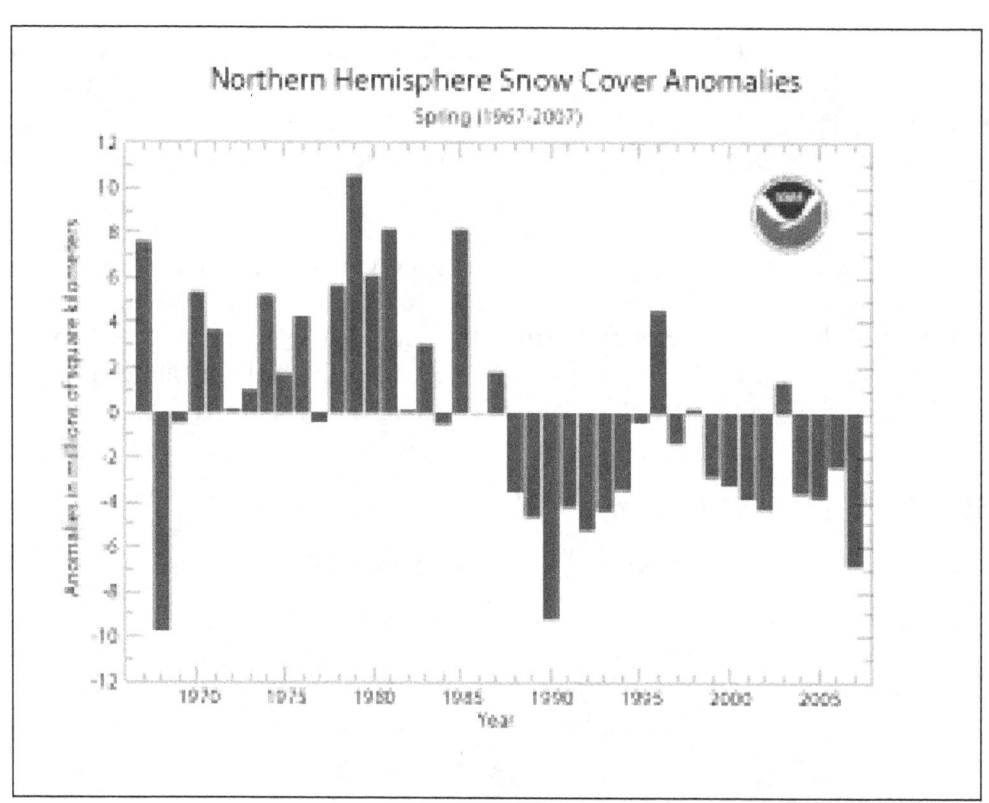

Figure 13. Northern Hemisphere snow cover anomalies for 1967–2007 spring (March–May).

Based on data through the end of the year, 2007 was the 10th warmest year on record for the U.S., with a nationally averaged temperature of 54.2°F (12.4°C). This value is 1.4°F (0.8°C) above the 20th century (1901–2000) mean (Figure 14).

Much-warmer-than-average temperatures affected much of the mountain west and parts of the east during 2007. This was the 10th warmest January–December in the 113-year record. Both Kentucky and Tennessee had the 4th warmest years on record. Forty-three of the lower 48 states were either warmer or much warmer than average in 2007. Maine alone ranked below average during the 2007 year-to-date period. The anomalous warmth affecting the U.S. in 2007 is also reflected in temperatures in the lower troposphere. Data collected by NOAA's TIROS-N polar-orbiting satellites and adjusted for time-dependent biases by NASA and the Global Hydrology and Climate Center at the University of Alabama in Huntsville indicate that temperatures in the lower half of the atmosphere (lowest 8 km of the atmosphere) over the U.S. were warmer than the 20-year (1979–1998) average for the 10th consecutive year.

Precipitation in the United States during 2007 was variable throughout much of the country, with periods of excessive rainfall, especially across the central third of the U.S., and persistent and developing drought in the southeastern quarter of the country and the far western states. Winter was relatively wet in the South and North Central regions and relatively dry in the West and Southeast (Figures 15 and 16). Spring was the driest March–May on record in the Southeast.

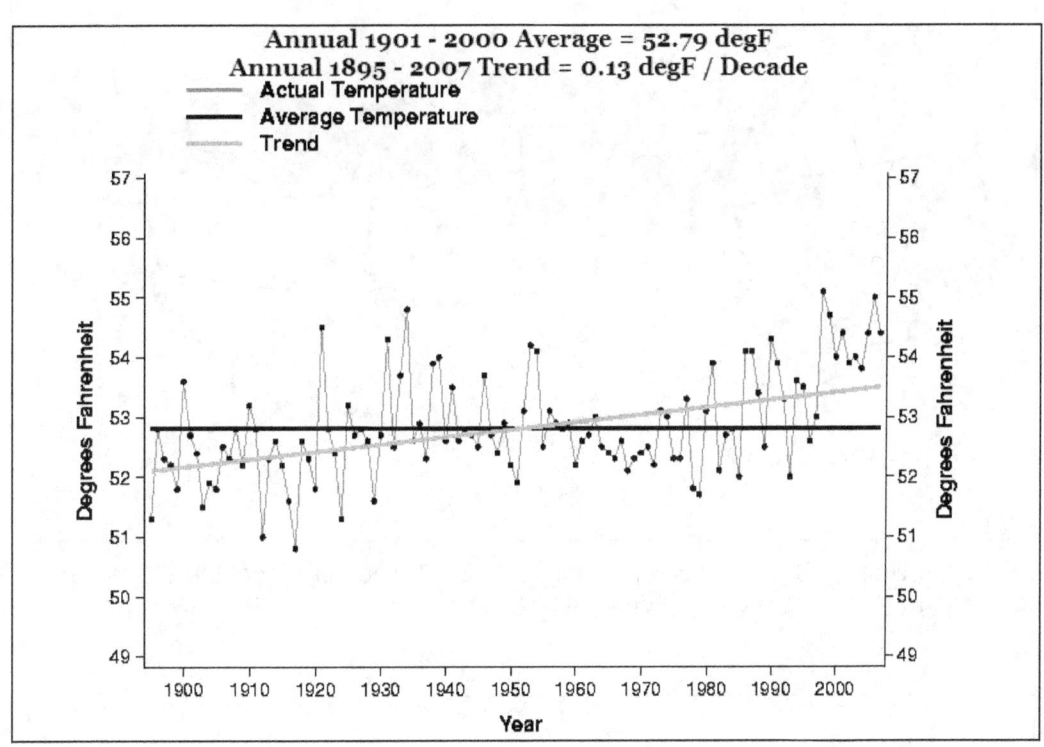

Figure 14. The long-term annual temperature trend for the United States based on the Historical Climate Network (HCN) which is a subset of the Cooperative Network of Weather Observers.

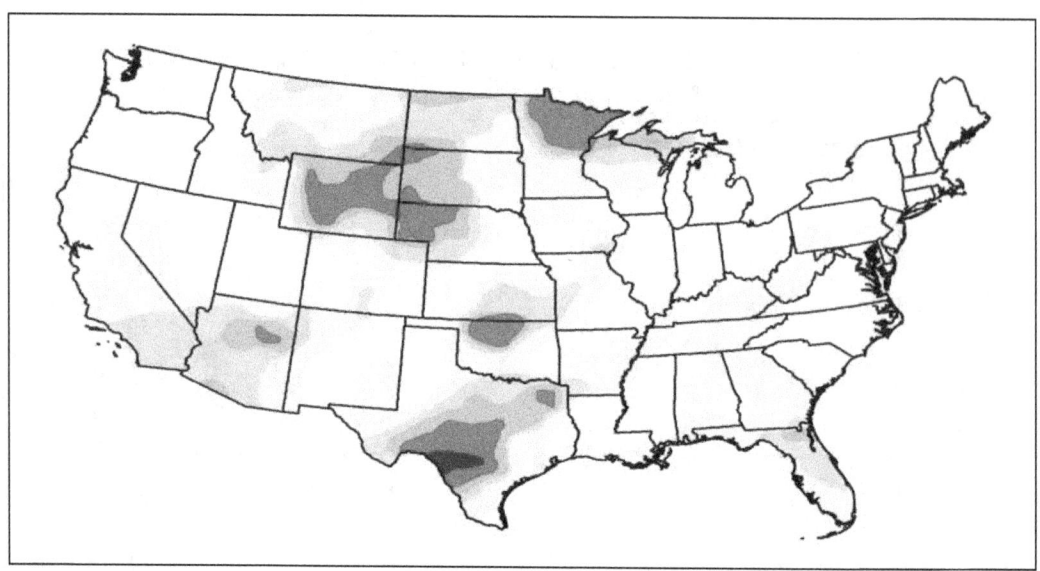

Figure 15. Palmer Drought Severity Index for January 2, 2007. The majority of the Plains were experiencing abnormally dry to moderate drought conditions.

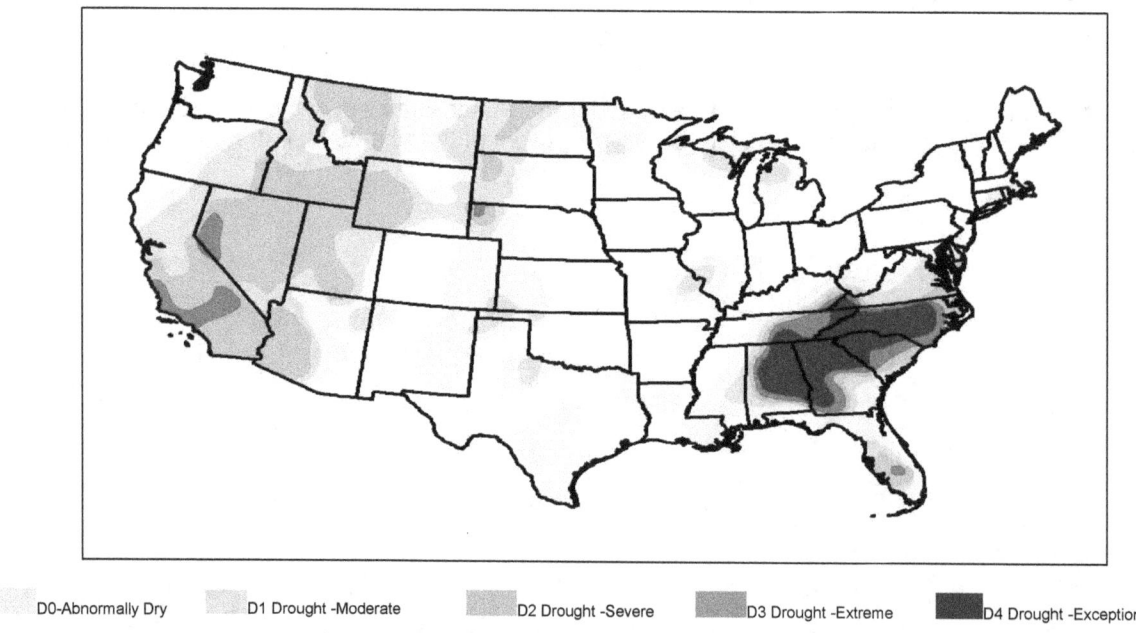

D0-Abnormally Dry   D1 Drought -Moderate   D2 Drought -Severe   D3 Drought -Extreme   D4 Drought -Exceptional

Figure 16. Palmer Drought Severity Index for December 25, 2007. The center of intensely dry weather had settled into the Southeast United States.

The West was ranked 6th driest and the West North Central region had its 3rd wettest spring on record. In summer, the remnants of Tropical Storm Erin brought excessive rain to Texas, Oklahoma, and Kansas, giving the South its wettest summer on record. Meanwhile, much of the Southeast continued to suffer in drought with its 11th driest summer on record, following the driest spring.

Precipitation across the U.S. during the fall ranked 37th driest, although no regions ranked much above or much below normal. For the contiguous U.S. as a whole, seven months in 2007 were drier than average. The annual temperature trend for the nation, based on the historical climate network (USHCN), shows that 2007 was down slightly from 2006 but still ranked as tied for the s6th warmest year in the past century.

Selected References

Davey, C. A., K. T. Redmond, and D. B. Simeral. 2007. Weather and Climate Inventory, National Park Service, Annual Climate Summary for 2004, Organ Pipe Cactus National Monument. Natural Resource Technical Report NPS/WASO/NRTR–2007. National Park Service, Fort Collins, Colorado.

Gelber, B. 2002. The Pennsylvania Weather Book. Rutgers University Press, New Brunswick, New Jersey.

Knight, P., T. Wisniewski, C. Bahrmann, and S. Miller. In preparation. Weather and Climate Monitoring Protocol for the Eastern Rivers and Mountains and Mid-Atlantic Networks. Natural Resource Report Series NPS/ERMN/NRR—2010/XXX. National Park Service, Fort Collins, CO.

Kocin, P. J., and L. W. Uccellini. 2004. Northeast Snowstorms Volume 1: Overview. Meteorological Monographs Vol 32, No 54. American Meteorological Society, Boston, Massachusetts.

Marshall, M. R., and N. B. Piekielek. 2007. Eastern Rivers and Mountains Network Ecological Monitoring Plan. Natural Resource Report NPS/ERMN/NRR—2007/017. National Park Service. Fort Collins, CO.

National Assessment Synthesis Team. 2001. Climate Change Impacts on United States: The Potential Consequences of Climate Variability and Change, Report for the U.S. Global Change Research Program. Cambridge University Press, Cambridge, UK.

National Oceanic and Atmospheric Administration (NOAA). 2007. National Climatic Data Center. Climate of 2007 – Annual Review, Global and U.S. Summary, http://lwf.ncdc.noaa.gov/oa/climate/research/2007/ann/us-summary.html.

Appendix

The following tables are a tally of all reports of severe weather during 2007 in the counties that encompass FONE and FRHI. These storm events were provided by the National Climatic Data Center (NCDC). NCDC receives this storm data from the National Weather Service, who acquires their information from a variety of sources. These sources include, but are not limited to county, state, and federal emergency management officials, local law enforcement officials, skywarn spotters, NWS damage surveys, newspaper clipping services, the insurance industry, and the general public. This Storm Data is an official publication of the National Oceanic and Atmospheric Administration (NOAA 2007), which documents the occurrence of storms and other significant weather phenomena having sufficient intensity to cause loss of life, injuries, significant property damage, and/or disruption to commerce. Each table contains the location, date, time, description of the severe event, its magnitude, and number of deaths, injuries, and property/crop damage associated with the event. The property and crop damage should be considered as a broad estimate.

Monongalia County

Location or County	Date	Time	Type	Mag	Dth	Inj	PrD	CrD
1 WVZ022	02/13/2007	09:00 AM	Ice Storm	N/A	0	0	0K	0K
2 Morgantown	02/21/2007	17:17 PM	Flash Flood	N/A	0	0	0K	0K
3 Star City	03/23/2007	19:00 PM	Flash Flood	N/A	0	0	0K	0K
4 Morgantown	04/01/2007	14:25 PM	Thunderstorm Wind	50 kts.	0	0	0K	0K
5 Morgantown	04/01/2007	17:05 PM	Flash Flood	N/A	0	0	1K	0K
6 Morgantown	06/08/2007	16:35 PM	Thunderstorm Wind	50 kts.	0	0	3K	0K
7 Morgantown	07/15/2007	17:40 PM	Thunderstorm Wind	50 kts.	0	0	5K	0K
8 Blacksville	07/29/2007	14:38 PM	Thunderstorm Wind	50 kts.	0	0	20K	0K
9 Westover	07/29/2007	14:38 PM	Thunderstorm Wind	50 kts.	0	0	20K	0K
10 Pursglove	08/09/2007	15:55 PM	Hail	1.00 in.	0	0	0K	0K
11 Morgantown	08/09/2007	16:00 PM	Thunderstorm Wind	50 kts.	0	0	30K	0K
12 Uffingtown	08/20/2007	14:45 PM	Thunderstorm Wind	50 kts.	0	0	25K	0K
13 Fieldcrest	08/21/2007	02:00 AM	Flood	N/A	0	0	2K	0K
14 Hagans	09/26/2007	20:55 PM	Thunderstorm Wind	50 kts.	0	0	30K	0K
15 Uffingtown	09/26/2007	21:10 PM	Hail	1.75 in.	0	0	0K	0K
16 Uffingtown	09/26/2007	21:10 PM	Thunderstorm Wind	50 kts.	0	0	30K	0K
17 WVZ022	12/05/2007	11:00 AM	Heavy Snow	N/A	0	0	0K	0K
18 Granville	12/13/2007	08:38 AM	Flood	N/A	0	0	20K	0K
				TOTALS:	0	0	186K	0

Mag: Magnitude; Dth: Deaths; Inj: Injuries; PrD: Property Damage; CrD: Crop Damage.

29

Fayette County

Location or County	Date	Time	Type	Mag	Dth	Inj	PrD	CrD
1 PAZ007 - 013>016 - 020>021 - 029>030 - 032	02/13/2007	08:00 AM	Heavy Snow	N/A	0	0	0K	0K
2 PAZ007 - 013>016 - 020>021 - 029>030 - 032	02/13/2007	08:00 AM	Ice Storm	N/A	0	0	0K	0K
3 PAZ032	03/07/2007	01:00 AM	Heavy Snow	N/A	0	0	0K	0K
4 PAZ032	04/16/2007	16:00 PM	Heavy Snow	N/A	0	0	0K	0K
5 Brownsville	06/08/2007	16:45 PM	Thunderstorm Wind	50 kts.	0	0	3K	0K
6 Fairchance	06/13/2007	14:45 PM	Hail	0.75 in.	0	0	0K	0K
7 Uniontown	06/13/2007	17:35 PM	Thunderstorm Wind	50 kts.	0	0	0K	0K
8 Grindstone	06/13/2007	18:00 PM	Thunderstorm Wind	50 kts.	0	0	0K	0K
9 Fayette City	06/21/2007	16:35 PM	Thunderstorm Wind	50 kts.	0	0	3K	0K
10 Connellsville	06/27/2007	16:19 PM	Thunderstorm Wind	50 kts.	0	0	0K	0K
11 Connellsville	06/27/2007	16:25 PM	Hail	0.88 in.	0	0	0K	0K
12 Connellsville	07/05/2007	14:25 PM	Flash Flood	N/A	0	0	50K	0K
13 Connellsville	07/19/2007	20:05 PM	Thunderstorm Wind	50 kts.	0	0	15K	0K
14 Smithfield	07/29/2007	13:31 PM	Hail	0.75 in.	0	0	0K	0K
15 Connellsville	08/07/2007	15:00 PM	Thunderstorm Wind	50 kts.	0	0	5K	0K
16 Perryopolis	08/07/2007	15:10 PM	Thunderstorm Wind	50 kts.	0	0	8K	0K
17 Dearth	08/08/2007	13:03 PM	Thunderstorm Wind	50 kts.	0	0	5K	0K
18 Everson	08/08/2007	13:03 PM	Hail	0.75 in.	0	0	0K	0K
19 Uniontown	08/09/2007	13:45 PM	Thunderstorm Wind	50 kts.	0	0	75K	0K
20 Leith	08/09/2007	15:00 PM	Flash Flood	N/A	0	0	25K	0K
21 Uniontown	08/09/2007	15:00 PM	Thunderstorm Wind	50 kts.	0	0	75K	0K
22 Brownsville	08/09/2007	15:18 PM	Flash Flood	N/A	0	0	50K	0K
23 Masontown	08/09/2007	16:25 PM	Hail	0.75 in.	0	0	0K	0K
24 Connellsville	08/09/2007	19:00 PM	Flash Flood	N/A	0	0	30K	0K
25 Newell	08/09/2007	19:00 PM	Flash Flood	N/A	0	0	10K	0K
26 Connellsville	08/09/2007	19:20 PM	Thunderstorm Wind	50 kts.	0	0	75K	0K
27 Leith	08/20/2007	17:40 PM	Thunderstorm Wind	50 kts.	0	0	60K	0K
28 Chalkhill	09/26/2007	22:10 PM	Thunderstorm Wind	52 kts.	0	0	0K	0K
29 Fayette City	12/14/2007	12:30 PM	Flood	N/A	0	0	5K	0K
				TOTALS:	0	0	494K	0

Mag: Magnitude; Dth: Deaths; Inj: Injuries; PrD: Property Damage; CrD: Crop Damage.

30

NPS 336/105513, 476/105513, September 2010

National Park Service
U.S. Department of the Interior

Natural Resource Program Center
1201 Oakridge Drive, Suite 150
Fort Collins, CO 80525

www.nature.nps.gov

EXPERIENCE YOUR AMERICA ™

www.ingramcontent.com/pod-product-compliance
Lightning Source LLC
Chambersburg PA
CBHW080928290526
45795CB00007BA/2681